A THIRTY-DAY EXPERIMENT IN PRAYER

A THIRTY-DAY EXPERIMENT IN PRAYER

Beginning a Prayer Journal

Robert Wood

THE UPPER ROOM
Nashville, Tennessee

A Thirty-Day Experiment in Prayer

First Printing, October, 1978 (8)
Second Printing, February, 1980 (5)
Third Printing, March, 1981 (5)

ISBN 0-8358-0380-5

Library of Congress Catalog Number: 78-65160

Printed in the United States of America

to my three girls
Rosemary, Stephanie, and Tracy
who always bring joy
to my prayer life

FOREWORD

Here is a travel book . . . for a month's journey into the habit of conversing with the Highest and Best, as you think and feel at the beginning and the end of a day of life, over a period of thirty days. (Thirty days is the classic time of testing one's self in a new mode of life.)

This book is an experiment in growing your own indigenous sensitivity.

The author does not tell you what to say for each prayer conversation, but does suggest that you read a Bible passage that may re-tune and start things going in your mind. Secondly, he shares his own dialogue with God at the end and the beginning of a robust day. And thirdly he suggest a plot for your own conversation with God toward a fresh creation of meanings-to-live. He does not give you a sermonette to recline upon, but like Kierkegaard, invites you to your own decisive thinking, conversation, and action—"upon which everything depends" if you are to be a truth bound in the bundle of the living with the Lord God.

The fourth step in this kind of prayer is to write—in memorable phrase and paragraph—the essential "root that is ever green" that you come to in this uncovering of the depths of your life. Name and let grow the liveness that comes up in your journey of spirit that morning or evening.

With this data increasingly before you, your understanding of yourself as human spirit trying to actualize (and evade) your possibilities in the actual world can cumulate and multiply its worth. Your consciousness will no longer spend so much time meandering over fields of withered fantasies and everydayness, but have consummations. The starts and stops, the bits and pieces, the ups and downs of your life journey can be connected with a thread of significance. Your name now has fresh character. So documented, the pulsing moods and lived moments of your life—and your consideration of them with God and the Holy Writ—can empower you to endure and to prevail. A prayer journal can function in your becoming human.

This is not a book to *read.* It's whole point is to develop a habit for you of regular conversation with the Highest and Best—while the immediacy of live events is still in your consciousness.

All that we know about the nature of a human being suggests the essentiality of a continuity in significant relationship, within which conversation about the world of our life can be regularly carried on. Without such conversation, an ordering of life that makes sense for any length of time, seems impossible. No one can construct a world to live in and the person-to-be with merely *private* consideration, talking merely to self. Why not, along with some significant others and our people's heritage, choose God as a continuing conversation partner—as we try to live as a human dignity?

A Prayer Journal is for the sake of a life style of *hilaritas* or cheerfulness . . . that He dwell in us and we in Him—communicatively. A Prayer Journal is for journey—

"Lead me in thy truth,
and teach me:
for thou
art the God of my salvation."

Ross Snyder

INTRODUCTION

WHY KEEP A JOURNAL?

Journal writing will help you put things in perspective. One of the images that comes quickly to mind as I try to explain what keeping a journal is, is a picture of a cow resting pleasantly under a shade tree in the middle of a pasture. As she lies there, gazing through half-opened eyes, chewing her cud, she is deeply immersed in the process that reminds me of journal writing. She has just spent hours busily grazing in the pasture, eating the grass, swallowing it. However, for that grass to be processed and result in milk, the cow must regurgitate that first eating, chew it again, and swallow it the second time to enter into her second stomach. Only then will the digestive process take place, and the original eating become life-sustaining milk. Keeping a journal is the process of digesting the spiritual meaning of the events of each day. These events have come with rapidity; they have come with feeling, some with thinking, some with just doing. Sometime during your hurried day you must take time out to reflect on the deeper significance of these events and to digest them into your own "life-sustaining milk." As you make sense of them, you will put them in perspective of their importance and lasting value to your own life.

A prayer journal enables you to take stock of the flood of sensations, feelings, and emotions you experience. It will increase the possibility of your being more fully conscious of the events in your life. It enables you to tune into yourself, tune into other persons, and tune into God through your feelings.

A journal is a way of caring—caring for and caring about. It is a way of caring for the important things in life and caring about your relationship to those important things.

Keeping a journal is that process of trying to grasp what really happened in an experience. It is a process of finding out what the *phenomena* (apparent experience including all the senses) of the experience is. You should record the experience or event exactly as it happened with you on the inside, and not as a bystander.

A journal has allowed me an opportunity to reflect on those moments of doing good and their relationship to the "eternal good."

One of the major reasons that I began keeping a journal myself was that it provided me an opportunity to reflect on my relationship with those things eternal. Let me explain. All of us from time to time experience those events in our lives which are our attempts to do good. In reflecting on a moment of joy, I would put this in perspective to the "eternal joy." In reflecting on a moment of suffering, I would put this in perspective to the one suffering that was necessary for the salvation of humankind. Journal writing, for me, is a process of putting my life in perspective with what I understand the religious life to be. Therefore, I do not simply go through a process of reflecting on the events in my life, but I put them in perspective with what scripture tells me that life ought to be.

A journal helps you to see if you are still on the Way or sidetracked somewhere in some pleasant spot that has you deceived. There was a story about a man who was traveling through the countryside. As he traveled about, he kept encountering pleasant spots which were so enticing that he would stop and rest for a while. The only problem was that these pleasant spots so deceived him that he believed he was still on the way—proceeding on his journey. Changes, maturing, growth, and spiritual insight just do not happen, but they come about when one consciously desires them.

Keeping a journal is the process of putting things in perspective, of testing whether or not a particular experience reflects your being on the Way or seated somewhere in a pleasant spot, deceived that you are still on the Way.

CAN I EXPECT GROWTH IN FAITH AND PRAYER LIFE?

Journal writing is a way of reflecting on your own spiritual growth. The book of James may give us an insight here. "When the way is rough, your patience has a chance to grow" (James 1:3, TLB). Unless you have an opportunity to reflect on the "roughness" in your life, you may become disheartened and discouraged about your own attempts to live a good life. If you use this roughness as an opportunity for growth, you might mature in a new dimension in your personal growth.

A journal can open up the doors of your own inner self and allow you to get a full look at your own personal religion. When you reflect on your own identity, when you ask the religious significance of a personal choice, you are participating in keeping a journal.

This process helps you to see words on the pages of scriptures take flesh and blood and dwell among us. One can read about meekness and patience and joy in the scriptures, intellectually comprehending them. A journal enables you to name your own life activities as being patient and meek and full of joy, and in the process of so doing, you desire and seek those in your future activities. You and I do not live in anticipation of abstract terms. We live in anticipation of experienced patience and joy.

A prayer journal is writing your own drama. You do not live in the drama of another one's story. You must participate in the excitement of writing your own drama—of making sense out of the "lived" moments of your life, and testing them against your understanding of what the Way asks of you. You take the fabric of your life apart, thread by thread, testing it for strength against what is meant to be strength; testing joy against what you hope joy will be; testing your loving against the great imperatives of scripture.

Journal writing can take your lived moments and make sense of them. During any normal day, hundreds of things happen which you can recall. Some you would evaluate as being positive experiences; some you would evaluate as negative experiences. Some experiences you cause to happen. Others happen to you because of outside causes. Some have great significance to the course and direction you seek to take. Others have little significance. Yet, the kind of sense you make out of each of them determines the person who you are.

Whether or not you admit it, your life is a theological statement. It is a statement of your action and interaction with God. If you unthinkingly bounce from experience to experience, more than likely God is going to have little impact on your life. But as you screen, evaluate, and control your life's events, you are more conscious of God's presence. And as you live in God's presence, you have a greater opportunity to share that presence with other people. Furthermore, as you live in God's presence, you have greater opportunities to create the environments in which you and others find fulfillment.

A journal helps you become aware of what you do and why you do what you do. It helps you reflect on how you do things. However, it is more than just the past—it helps you project activities into the future and, in the process, come to an understanding of what the future holds for you in a religious sense. You constantly measure what you have done with alternate ways of thinking and doing the same events in the future. You have an opportunity to reflect on your world, on others, and your relationships to both of these. Keeping a journal is a process of viewing a drama and constantly rewriting the script for the next performance.

One of the benefits of keeping a journal is what I call, getting a glance at history. As you keep a journal, you begin to make graphic patterns of experiences in your life. As this history writing continues, the patterns of your life become more visible. If you formerly thought you were fairly stable, you may find a rhythm of fluctuation in your response/activities. If you formerly thought of yourself as being unstructured, you may find that your life is highly structured. If you formerly thought of yourself as being conservative or liberal, you may find the opposite view as you delineate the experiences and place a value system on those experiences. In essence, you will find out that there may be a difference between what you think your values are and the values that you actually live by.

Keeping a journal is an effective process of enabling you to see things from where you stand. This is a very necessary step in the process of changing and selecting a value system to live by. As you truly seek to grow spiritually and become involved in the process of journal writing, you may bring to life the scripture that says, "Now we see in a mirror dimly, but then face to face." As you reflect on the experience, you may be able to see the threads that went together to weave the cloth of that experience.

A prayer journal provides you an opportunity of gaining new strengths, new insights, and new affirmations of your personal call to be one of Christ's disciples. It is not a secret formula for making you a more mature Christian. But, as in many things, it will become more meaningful to the degree that you put yourself to the task of making sense of God's participation in your life. Just as the word *disciple* itself connotes, keeping a journal provides you an opportunity of learning more about the Christian Way. By testing and measuring your life in the context of the Christian witness, you become a part of the community of faith.

WHAT GOES INTO MY JOURNAL?

Those who keep a diary already have a basic understanding of journal writing. Most diaries are very small and, therefore, mandate the keeping of only those significant events in one's life. You should be selective as to what you put into your journal. Those events during the day which made an impact and are still vibrating within you should be the content for that day's journal entry. Before writing anything in a journal, think back over your entire day and pick out one or two encounters, either with someone else or with yourself, that made a significant impact on your memory. Think in poetic and symbolic language before writing, making sure that you capture all the feelings and emotions of the participants.

Then, as you begin to retell these events, try to make your description as graphic as the original experience. You may choose never to share these with anyone else. Should you choose to do so, you would want this telling to create in them all the same feelings and emotions and insights as the original experience brought to you. When you first begin to write about the day's activities, simply try to tell the story in all its vividness without moralizing or reflecting. Then, once the event is told, begin the second process of making sense of that event. This can be done in perspective of past events or by relational reflection with scriptures or other sources of eternal truth.

As a beginning experience in journal keeping, I suggest you make a graph of your religious experience. We come to a Christian commitment from a variety of religious experiences. Some of those we would describe as mountaintop experiences. Other experiences are similar to the valley described in Psalm 23. The task of religious maturity is not to stop this fluctuation from mountaintop and valley, but rather, to log and make sense of the experience itself. Once you properly evaluate your peak experiences, you can diligently seek to repeat them more frequently in your own life.

Take a piece of graph paper, and on the left side, mark "Birth," and on the right side, mark "Today." On the top of the page put a plus sign and on the bottom, put a minus sign. Then, as you move from "birth" to "today," try to identify those chronological points which stand out in your mind as being moments of deep faith or great turmoil. Consider such points as: your family relationships, your experiences in the church, high points of summer camps, your college or work experience, your decision to get married or remain single, the decision to have children or consider others as your children, your decision to join the church or take a certain responsibility in the church, or your decision to become involved in various ministries. These are merely suggestions. You may have many other high moments and low moments which stand out in your mind as expressions of your own particular faith. You should keep in mind that the graph is not a grading system to see whether or not you have more pluses than minuses, but an honest evaluation of your own religious experiences.

You may want to consider keeping a graph on selected days. Begin the same process from the time that you awaken to the time that you sit down to take stock of the day's activities. This graphic picture will help you look at various aspects of your day's journey. As you become open and more secure in this process, you may want to share this graph with loved ones or a small group of friends. This is very meaningful if they, too, are in the process of keeping a journal of their religious experiences.

CAN I KEEP MY JOURNAL PRIVATE?

Journal writing should not be considered a process of self-exposure. This is a process that is totally private if you choose to make it so. There are no test scores; you will not be graded. This journal is only self-exposure to the degree that you are able to see yourself as you truly are.

HOW DO I GET STARTED?

Let me suggest some simple alternatives for you to use as stimulus for making your entries into your journal. First of all, review your day:

What moments did you feel closest to Christ?

What moment during the day did you feel you were responding to God's call to be his disciple?

Where did you participate in "being the church" this day?

When was your faith tested this day? Was it tested through failure or success?

What is your plan for tomorrow so that you can be Christ's disciple?

You might want to review the three following areas as possibilities for helping you to reflect on your walk with Christ during the day. They are:

Your Spiritual Life
Your Study
Your Action

Your Spiritual Life—"You shall worship the Lord with your whole heart." Consider your morning devotion, your prayer life, worship attendance, communion, or any other devotional activities that might have been particularly meaningful for you.

Your Study—"The truth shall make you free." Did you realize God's presence through reading scripture or your daily devotional guide? Were your horizons brightened through reading religious publications, denominational newsletters, or religious magazines? Did you come to some new religious understanding while attending a Bible study, a church school class, or a religious seminar?

Your Action—"I will make you fishers of men." What have you done this day so that Christ was better known and lived in your family, your vocation, your community, and your church?

As you go through this 30-day experiment, the prayers for morning and evening are "thought starters" that can provide you a format for reflecting on your day's experience. As you read the prayers and the scripture and participate in the activities suggested, you may be called to a fresh awareness of your lived moments. A conscious effort to achieve a particular task can provide an opportunity of a fresh awareness of the vitality of that particular activity.

WHAT KIND OF OUTCOME CAN I EXPECT?

Jesus said, "If you continue in my word, you are truly my disciples, and you will know the truth, and the truth will make you free" (John 8:31-32, RSV). It has been said that truth does not consist in us knowing it, but in being that truth. This seems to be the heart of what Jesus is sharing with us. Being a Christian, a disciple in Jesus' words, does not consist in affirming any particular truth, but in being that truth. Keeping a journal is that process that allows you to truly realize that you have been a "truth" in the midst of your existence. Truth is not the result of your activities, but a presence in the midst of your activities. A journal provides you with the possibility of seeing Christ in yourself—those moments when you have participated in contemporary revelation.

Please do not misunderstand me. No one achieves these goals all the time. Following Jesus' resurrection he found his disciples back at their nets. Being a Christian is more of an attitude of availability, and journal writing enables you to test your availability to the presence of Christ in your lives and the lives of others, and in the activities of your world.

Capable for Love

READ: 1 Corinthians 13
Psalm 8

Father in heaven,
The psalmist says that we are made a little less than God.
But for what are we made, O God?
We have
walked on the moon, talked with Mars;
split the atom and put it together again;
rechanneled rivers and moved mountains;
changed climates and reshaped bodies.
But for what purpose, Lord?
To say that *we* did it?
We pray, Lord, give us humility.
In this quiet prayer time, speak to us of another miracle, the miracle of love.
Why do I look for your revelation in the spectacular and the unusual, when all the time I walk knee-deep in the miracle of love?
Acts of renewing, forgiving, and reconciling are deeply rooted in your Spirit.
Send me forth this day, equipped with your Spirit and your love.
Make me capable of love, and revealing your love. Amen.

REFLECTION/ACTION

"Love does not insist on its own way." Is it possible to love someone without expecting anything in return? What makes it possible or not possible to love someone this way? Can I do an act of love today without expecting something in return?

Morning—Day One

Stoplights

READ: Psalm 91

Father God,
Why is it that I think I must get somewhere, assume some position, be gathered together, or separated apart in the quiet of my study to pray?
Why is it that I feel that I have to go somewhere or do some particular act to find you, reach you, and talk with you?
Your presence is here
in the city—on the busy bus, in the factory, in the cockpit of the airplane;
in the hospital—in the patients' rooms, in the intensive care unit, in the waiting room;
in the home—at dinner, in the bedroom, in the family room, at my work bench;
in the car—in the parking lot, at the stoplight.
Lord, reveal your presence to me everywhere, and help me become aware of your presence each moment of the day.
May your presence fill the nonanswers, empty glances, and lonely times of my life. Amen.

REFLECTION/ACTION

During this thirty-day experience, I will try to develop the practice of stoplight prayers—while waiting at stoplights (be they real traffic lights or moments like waiting for a dialed phone to ring, a doorbell to be answered, an elevator to reach my floor, or a three-minute egg to cook). I will reflect in my journal on those experiences and moments when I was aware of being in God's presence.

Evening—Day One

Praising God

READ: Paul's letter to Philemon
"I pray that the sharing of your faith may promote the knowledge of all the good that is ours in Christ" (Philemon, verse 6, RSV).

Lord, this morning is a glorious day.
It is another day when I can praise and give thanks for all the things you have done for me and all your children.
You have created me free and given me my freedom.
I do not mean freedom from
job, family, the call, carpool, spouse, and children, responsibility, maturity, choices, love, and hope.
But I mean you have given me freedom to
have jobs, raise families, join organizations, answer the call, and love my spouse and children.
I can make choices which enhance the experience of responsibility and freely choose between alternatives which enable maturity.
You have given me freedom for the future which brings me hope and anticipation.
Lord, you have sent your Spirit which freely equips me for freedom.
Let me be your witness of freedom this day, that all will see the good that is ours in Christ.
It is in his name I pray. Amen.

REFLECTION/ACTION

What is the difference between my love and God's love being acted out through me? With whom do I feel estranged? What can I do to share God's love with that person?

Morning—Day Two

Give Thanks!

READ: Psalm 30

Dear Lord,

What is it in me that always looks at the problems and never at the opportunities in life?

Help me change my outlook on life and see the good in life that is at your hands.

When I see a small child, tearfully in the corner, help me give thanks and take time to change the tear to a smile.

When I see a vagrant, let me not curse the dark and walk on the other side of the street, or turn my back.

Help me give thanks and witness to things eternal in my life and possible for his life.

When I see a lonely widow, grieving her life away over her loved one, let me not curse the world who has turned its back on her.

Help me give thanks and reach out with your love, for surely your love can be the answer.

When I see the tender exchange between a mother and child, help me give thanks.

There is much in the world for which to give thanks.

The joy we have found in you is eternal.

Let me see opportunities for sharing that joy. Amen.

REFLECTION/ACTION

What was today like? Was it possible to love someone with the love of God? Was I God's agent of love? What am I thankful for today?

Evening—Day Two

[illegible]

[illegible]

Me

READ: Genesis 2:4b-7
2 Corinthians 4:1-5, 5:10

Dear Lord,
What is this thing called me?
Am I a curious mixture of clay and breath, of flesh and spirit, of movement and thought, of remembering and hope?
Sometimes I am able to get outside of myself and get away from myself.
Sometimes I can do anything with myself . . . I surprise myself.
There is a part of me that is dying because I deny the gifts of grace you have shared with me.
There is a part of me that is renewing—day by day.
I am renewed inwardly by your Spirit;
I am nourished by the fruits of the earth;
my mind and body replenish their cells.
Lord, help me understand that troubles are the stimulus for the answers of your Spirit; our troubles are slight and short-lived compared to the eternal joy of your glory.
Teach me to call on your Spirit and to discipline my body so I will be able to run the long race, and fight the good fight.
Could it be that you are calling on me for such a revelation?
Amen.

REFLECTION/ACTION

What are my possibilities for renewal of my physical being through exercise and renewal of my spiritual being through prayer?

Morning—Day Three

Brothers and Sisters in Christ

READ: Philippians 1:1-11

Today, Lord,
Someone called me his brother in Christ.
It puzzled me at first.
This man is not usually very brotherly, loving, friendly, supportive, or trusting.
What can I expect of a brother or sister in Christ?
My brothers do not always agree with me.
They are not always kind in their criticism of me.
Sometimes
they insist on their own way;
they have the wildest ideas;
they have the simplest ideas.
But regardless of the situation, the meeting, or the decision, they are there to help.
I guess that is it, Lord.
Brothers and sisters in Christ—
are there to help.
They share in your gift of discernment.
Thank you, Lord, for this gift of the Spirit.
My brothers and sisters in Chist know how to measure my needs—encouragement, support, enthusiasm, challenge, resistance, or plain *no.*
The love of your Spirit is so perceptive.
It knows when, where, and how;
so that together we may be richer
in knowledge and insight of every kind. Amen.

REFLECTION/ACTION

Could beginning something new that would equip me for the ministry of Jesus Christ change my life? How can I enlist a group of my friends to become vital, active participants in the ministry of Christ?

Evening—Day Three

In the Valley

READ: Psalm 23
Ephesians 2:1-10

Father God,
Thank you for calling me to the valley.
The valley seems dark and fearsome with
problems of injustice,
misunderstandings and frustration,
injury, pain, and mental anguish.
Problems of this world may loom large in my eyes and heavy on my heart; but once again I read, "I will not be afraid, for you are with me."
Renewal is your promise.
Your Spirit shall renew me with
mercy to face injustice,
truth to face misunderstandings,
wisdom to face frustration,
healing to face injury and pain,
friends to face mental anguish.
Goodness and unfailing love will follow me in your valley, all the days of my life.
So I can
boast and brag,
perform miracles,
be raised above my brothers and sisters.
Not so, but for the purpose of dwelling in your house and being your instrument of truth, wisdom, healing, and love in the valley.
Thank you, Lord, for such glorious work. Amen.

REFLECTION/ACTION

Today I stopped along my journey: to consider God's plan for me as I became aware of flowers and friends. The valley of life is frightening for me. There are times when I am convinced that there is no comfort and that I really am alone. Why do I feel that way? How can I become more aware of God and his comforting presence?

Morning—Day Four

Timing

READ: Ecclesiastes 3:1-15

Almighty God,
Teach me timing.
Not the kind used for cars, music, or clocks.
Teach me the kind of timing needed for life in Christ.
Turn, turn, turn.
The world turns in haste. Seldom do I find the time for things of eternal value.
Lord, teach me the seasons, the time for everything under the heavens.
There are times in my life to plant
an idea in the mind of an inquisitive child,
a seed of hope for someone in need,
the gift of trust in one birthing faith.
There are times in our lives
to scatter stones that build walls,
to gather stones that build bridges between alienated individuals.
Teach us the times to seek
out the fellowship of the body of Christ,
the solitude of meditation,
to serve others with humility and love.
For every activity—silence, speech, mourning, dancing, weeping, laughing, tearing, mending, loving, and hating—for all these things we praise you.
Help us use them to know your work in the world and our calling to that work. Amen.

REFLECTION/ACTION

Where did God share the "immeasurable riches of his grace in kindness" through me today? What is my life like right now? How does today fit into my journey?

Evening—Day Four

Agents of Peace

READ: Romans 14
Ephesians 6:10-20

Father in heaven,
As I awake this morning and look out over the snow-covered yard with the sun rising in a glistening ball of fire, can there be anything more peaceful?
Is peace the absence of war?
Or is peace the unity established between people as they seek and strive for common good?
Is peace the absence of sound?
Or is peace the pain of healing, the exercise necessary to heal a broken body or spirit?
Lord, touch me with your Spirit in this moment, so that this day I can be your agent of peace. Let me take your peace to the breakfast table, to my children's waking moments, to the goodbye kiss with my spouse, to the office, and to every encounter I make this day.
Allow me to experience no boundaries in sharing your peace with the happy, sad, joyful, needful, confident,
and yearning people of my day.
Let all my days find the reward of peace. Amen.

REFLECTION/ACTION

What is peace? Can I be God's agent for peace? Am I able to involve myself in both the activity and passivity of peace?

Morning—Day Five

Guidance

READ: Proverbs 8:1-11
1 Thessalonians 5:1-11

Eternal and ever-present God,
This has been one heck of a day.
I come to you this evening concerned about guidance.
Guidance is so important in our lives.
Teach me to be firm
  with people; with my children.
Teach me
  firmness that teaches maturity and responsibility,
  firmness with the unbeliever that shares faith and not arrogance.
Teach me the time to be accepting of people.
Teach me acceptance that
  affirms people;
  portrays affirmation and not valuelessness;
  gives direction and not license;
  displays my willingness to become a part of things and not an uninvolved judge.
Teach me the time to be loving
  the loving that comes from you,
  the loving that displays the will of God and not simply the human will,
  the loving that brings peace and security and not turmoil.
Guide me, Lord God, so that my heart can beat with the pulse of your will for all humankind. Amen.

REFLECTION/ACTION

How am I involved in being God's agent of peace? What will it take to create an atmosphere of peace?

Evening—Day Five

Being A Witness for Christ

READAD: Joshua 24:14-15
Acts 1:1-8

Dear Lord,
As I start this day,
help me focus my mind and spirit on you;
make me go about as if I am wearing a pair of glasses, so that I can see everything through you;
help me choose you;
help me be your witness in the world.
Make me witness for you, Christ, in every moment. In times of joy when my friends find some new moments of maturity, help me to remember the foundation of mature actions.
In moments of agony and pain of loss or setback, guide me to you for security and support.
In heart-to-heart dialogue, remind me to enrich my conversation with the cement of your love.
In decision and resolution, enable me to be your witness to the foundation of all deciding.
When authority is being tested and people are challenging or setting the course of history, direct me to be your witness and share the authority of eternity.
When people are claiming pride in their ancestors, enable me to remember the roots of my heritage, the God of Abraham and Jacob.
In moments of pride, make me not be prideful of my accomplishments, but witness to the accomplishments made by you, through me.
Day by day, minute by minute, opportunity by opportunity, give me the strength and presence of mind to witness. Amen.

REFLECTION/ACTION

Do I take the time and opportunity to be a witness for Christ? Have I shared with someone how a life in Christ will bring lasting fulfillment?

Morning—Day Six

Neighbors

READ: 2 Corinthians 5:16-21

Father God,
I come to you this evening, my mind cluttered with neighbors.
I cannot get them out of my mind; help me deal with them.
I am concerned with the neighbor constantly wanting to do something for me.
She has a great capacity to do, to love, and to help;
but Lord, I just do not need that much doing, loving, and helping.
Teach me the patience to understand and to channel her energy into your ministry. Only there will she find eternal fulfillment.
I am concerned with the neighbor who is lonely.
Sometime, somewhere in his life, his self-esteem has been injured, people have walked out on him.
Send your Spirit enabling me to touch his spirit and quicken him to an understanding that he is "created a little less than the angels."
I am concerned about the teenager next door who just got thrown out of his home, his clothes thrown on the street.
I have had great trouble meeting and getting to know his parents.
Show me a way to bring healing to this family.
I want to celebrate with the neighbor who has just gotten a new promotion, or a new child by adoption, or a wedding announcement, or another year older.
There have been times in my life when my spirit was lifted because of achievement and success.
Make me mindful of the real basis of celebration and success.
My mind is cluttered with thoughts of my neighbors.
Thank you for giving me a faith that teaches me to "love thy neighbors as thyself." Amen.

REFLECTION/ACTION

Was it easy to be a witness for God in Christ Jesus? How have I shared my church, scripture, Christ, or personal faith with others? How have I put my faith and life together?

Evening—Day Six

READ: Psalm 49:12, 16
Genesis 2[illegible]

Heavenly Father,
Direct me in one objective this day—to make you first in my life.
I thought in the morning I attended only to physical needs:
I went to the bathroom and the shower,
I came to the breakfast table,
I [illegible] dressed in [illegible] clothes.
I also consider my intellectual needs in the morning,
going to the front door for the newspaper,
listening to the news while I shaved,
reading *Time* at the breakfast table.
But somewhere along the way I ran into trouble, [illegible]
[illegible] I passed a church,
and I remembered.
Lord, help me to pray.
Lord, help me to put first things first.
I do have physical needs, emotional needs, and intellectual needs.
But my deepest needs are spiritual.
It is the spirit that integrates, coordinates, and enables all my being to love,
Through the Spirit I am able to love with the love of God.
Only when I put first things first do I love [illegible] with the love of God.
Help me to live this day, with you first in my life, enabling me to put first things first. Amen.

REFLECTION/ACTION

The well-integrated person might be defined as having the spiritual, the emotional, and the physical in harmony. These three levels are bound up in and influenced by one another. The physical is the lowest [illegible], the spirit [illegible] the most essential. Unless a value order is preserved, we are perverted.
Success comes when we get these levels in order. What will it take to meet [illegible] of these needs so that I am aware of their real importance?

First Things, First

READ: 1 John 4:7-12, 16
Genesis 24:12a

Heavenly Father,
Direct me in one objective this day—to make you first in my life.
Too often in the morning I consider only my physical needs.
I rush to the bathroom and the shower;
I rush to the breakfast table;
I rush to get dressed in coordinated colors.
I also consider my intellectual needs in the morning—
rushing to the front door for the newspaper,
listening to the news while I shave,
reading *Time* at the breakfast table.
But somewhere along the way I run into trouble, or a fellow Christian, or pass a church.
And I remember.
Lord, help me to pray.
Lord, help me to put first things, first.
I do have physical needs, emotional needs, and intellectual needs.
But my first needs are spiritual.
It is the Spirit that integrates, coordinates, and enables all my being to love.
Through the Spirit I am able to love with the love of God.
Only when I put first things, first, do I love completely with the love of Christ.
Help me to live this day, with you first in my life, enabling me to put first things, first. Amen.

REFLECTION/ACTION

The well-integrated person might be defined as having the spiritual, the emotional, and the physical in harmony. These three levels are bound up in and influenced by one another. The physical is the least noble of the three, the spiritual the most exalted. Unless a value-order is preserved, we are perverted.
Success comes when we get these levels in order. What will it take to meet all of these needs, so that I am aware of their real importance?

Morning—Day Seven

The Great Hunt

READ: 1 Thessalonians 5:12-24

Father God,
This week I have undertaken a search something like a great hunt.
I cannot remember when I have looked so hard for you.
I have looked for you in
  my decisions,
  my family,
  my business desk,
  the seasons,
  the needs of my neighbors,
  the quiet chapel.
But you know something, Lord?
In all my searching, in all my looking, I have not found you once.
You have found me every time.
Now I know the meaning of the hound of heaven.
You, God, are constantly seeking me out to share your love and light.
In all my seeking, I find you looking me square in the eyes.
You come around the corners of my life, seeking me out and never letting go of my life.
You call me to be your disciple.
Thank you, Lord, for the great hunt. Amen.

REFLECTION/ACTION

Has God been finding me, as I have sought to find him? Are new patterns emerging in my life? Am I doing some things differently? Are there some new directions and decisions that I should make as a part of my life?

Evening—Day Seven

Watchpersons

READ: Psalm 130
Matthew 13:10-17

Dear Lord,
Out of a deep sleep I have called to you.
As I awake, where have I been?
Was I far away from you? How near to you was I?
Was I aware of your presence? Did I tremble with fear?
I realize there is no place that I could go where you would not be near me.
You are always near me.
in my decisions
in my actions
in my nonaction
in my emotion
in my nonresponse.
You are near me when I walk
in the inner city,
across the meadow and cornfield.
You are there
in my response of love to my children,
in my concerned action to a young girl, lost
and estranged.
You breathe advice and support to meet all needs.
You point me to scriptural comfort that brings both a tear and a sigh of relief.
Lord, speak to those
who are lost,
who love,
who seem only to disbelieve.
Speak that all, whatever their need, might hear.
Speak to me. Amen.

REFLECTION/ACTION

How has God spoken to me in events, people, and issues? Will I act when I have heard God's call?

Morning—Day Eight

Full Measure

READ: Daniel 2:27
1 Corinthians 4:1-5

Father,
Thank you for this day.
Today you introduced me to "a little old man." He was a wonderful man.
As I looked into his eyes, it was like meeting his soul, face to face.
Each of his words imparted wisdom, and every gesture was a recollection of history.
His stories of love reflect your Spirit. The warmth of his smile reminded me of brotherhood.
It seemed that he shared a lifetime of insight in just one visit.
As we departed, he shared these words, "Find your full measure." Or did he say, "Be your full measure." "Give your full measure?" It makes no difference.
I know what he meant.
Your Son is our measure.
First we must find him, then we must live in him, and finally we must give that measure to everyone.
In every place I go and with everyone I meet, Lord, help me to meet your full measure.

REFLECTION/ACTION

If I heard God speaking to me today, did I respond? How has my experience of God made me grow and change?

Evening—Day Eight

Teach Me to Pray

READ: Matthew 6:5-16

Eternal Father,
Teach me to pray,
For I, like the disciples who asked Jesus, have been exposed to so much bad prayer.
So much prayer is people standing in public places calling attention to themselves, their causes, their successes.
Here in the quiet of my room teach me to say—
"Father God who dwells in places eternal."
Your name, Yahweh, speaks of life itself.
I pray that your kingdom is where I live, and I pray that your good is always my good.
Give me love to share, maturity to lead, and wisdom to make the right choices.
Forgive me for the times I loved myself, played the fool, judged for gain.
Do not let me count the wrongs against myself.
Send your Spirit upon me that I might be guarded against evil.
The highest goal for my life is your kingdom.
My desire is to bring glory to you. Amen.

REFLECTION/ACTION

How is prayer significant to reaching the goal of God's kingdom? Is prayer significant in my life? Where is God's kingdom in my life?

Morning—Day Nine

Reveal

READ: John 14:1-14

Lord,
Where should I look for you?
My day is all filled with much to do—
with love,
with hate,
with encounters that go nowhere.
My emotions are touched by a child from Uganda, the laughing of my Aunt Bess, the cries of a lonely world, the clumsiness of big government, the potential of big government.
My hope is stirred by the promise of youth, reading the Gospels, the acts of love I see, the acts of justice I see, your acts of mercy I know.
I question my future when I see outbursts of anger between people and among nations.
My life is refreshed by notes of celebrating songs, and by the sun shining through clouds of terror.
But, Lord, the question still haunts me, "Where should I look for you?" "Where are you trying to reveal yourself to me?"
Am I seeing this wrong?
Should I be asking, "Where am I trying to reveal you—
your love, justice, and mercy?
Help me to be your spokesman. Amen.

REFLECTION/ACTION

Where has God been visible in my life? Was I aware of God's presence? What did it feel like to be consciously aware of God's presence?

Evening—Day Nine

Bloom Where You Are Planted

READ: Matthew 6:25-34

Father God,
People are a funny lot.
We scurry around trying to improve our plight, always looking for a better flower bed.
We act as if we, with all our effort, could pull up our roots, and find some new fertile soil—perfect with fertilizer and moisture.
We seem to think that good soil is just waiting for us to capitalize on its environment.
There is something wrong with that kind of situation.
Shouldn't we seek to bloom where we are planted?
If the soil somewhere else is fertile, hasn't someone else done the work to make it so?
Is the fertile soil not the fruits of someone else who has given their life in the tilling?
What right have I to rush in and harvest the fruits of their life's labor?
Lord, set me to the task of plowing the furrow straight, deep, and carefully.
When I am plowing, keep me from disturbing those plants that are about to bloom themselves.
But with this little plot of ground you have given me, let me
nurture it for growth,
cultivate it with care,
lavish it with love.
Lord, give me the patience to wait for your blooming in my life.
Help me to feel comfortable where I am.
Give me confidence that you will use me, and help me bloom where I am planted. Amen.

REFLECTION/ACTION

Is the grass always greener somewhere else? Does patience or impatience prevail over my activities? As I practice patience and listen for God to guide me, can I allow God's will to be done and not my own?

Morning—Day Ten

Tiptoes

READ: Ephesians 4:1-16

Holy Father,
Remembering can be a sweetness in life.
Today, for some reason I found myself remembering events from my childhood.
I remembered when I was a small boy, in the midst of Oklahoma.
I would go about with my cattle-tending Dad.
I remember standing on tiptoes to see over the top rail of a feed lot.
I also stood on tiptoes to see the new purchases when we went shopping.
Lord, when was the last time I stood on tiptoes—
   stretching to see over the horizon,
   stretching to see tomorrow,
   stretching to see the cutting edge of life?
Many times I am complacent and view life from my easy chair.
I am content to let life come to me, taking whatever comes, no matter what I must deal with.
Lord, shock me out of my easy chair.
Holy Spirit, get me up on my tiptoes again; put me on the frontiers of your revelation.
As a revealer, help me affirm my faith.
As a witness, make me share your truth.
As a disciple, help me share your love.
As your servant, help me accept your suffering.
As your child, let me share eternity.
God, I thank you for tiptoe experiences. Amen.

REFLECTION/ACTION

How well did I practice patience and listen for God today? How difficult was it? What has God revealed to me and through me that makes me positive he is active in both my life and the world? What does it mean to have received a special gift, making me part of the body of Christ in the world?

Evening—Day Ten

Not of the World

READ: Luke 9:23-27

This morning, Lord, I woke up thinking, "Be in the world, but not of the world."
That is a constant struggle for me.
As I live in the world, what do I put first?
The world is full of
decisions,
television and newspapers,
P.T.A. meetings,
the stock market,
children and spouses,
friends.
What influences me to put certain things first?
Do I let myself become a victim of circumstances, allowing the world to set my priorities?
Is that what being *of* the world means?
Lord, I pray that you will become more real to me, so I may be *in* the world rather than *of* the world.
Strengthen every area of my life.
Help me realize the wonderful potential you share with each of your children.
Awaken in me my fullest potential to love, answer, ask, and share with you and others.
Lord, I pray that you become more real to me so I can be *in* the world.
Make me your window in the world, so others can see, share, and trust you in setting their priorities.
Enable all of us to be in the world, but not of the world. Amen.

REFLECTION/ACTION

How do I set my priorities? How do I feel my priorities should be set? Does God's will come first when I set my priorities?

Morning—Day Eleven

Others

READ: Titus 3:1-11

Father God,
Sometimes my world becomes so small that I seem to be the only one in it.
Help me to push back the walls.
Help me to stretch the horizons of my world and include all of your children in it.
In my smallness, Lord, I pray to you, concerned only about my individual needs.
Tonight, help me consider the needs of others.
Make me become more aware of my responsibility to rely heavily on your Spirit to bring other persons the good news.
I have experienced your grace through
the love of my children,
renewed strength in face of need,
the fellowship of your community,
the breaking of the bread and taking of the cup.
Experiencing your grace I have a responsibility to share your grace.
Help me make it evident that it is your grace I seek to share.
Help me become comfortable and verbal about what your love has done in my life, and what it can do in the lives of everyone.
Lord, let my wisdom speak your being, my attitudes share your love, my living display your blessings, my brotherhood portray the life of Jesus, and my rejoicing reflect his resurrection.
It is in his name I pray. Amen.

REFLECTION/ACTION

As I set my priorities today, have I kept God and others in mind? How difficult has it been to reorder priorities?

Evening—Day Eleven

New

READ: Revelations 21:1-7

Lord,
When I was a small boy, my family did not have very much in worldly possessions.
I can remember one time when I received a new bicycle.
It was new and it was all mine.
What excitement!
But eventually the newness wore off that bicycle.
The paint faded, the tires went flat, the seat became scuffed, and my excitement waned over the "new bicycle."
There have been other new things in my life—
a new house, new job, new car, new child.
All have brought excitement and change to my life.
There is one *new* that has brought more change, more fulfillment, and more excitement than all the rest.
That *new* is a new start, a new start in my faith.
Faith in Jesus Christ gave me a new start.
Unencumbered by memory of sin
I could start with new brush strokes
to paint the beauty of life, lived in the midst
of your grace.
Lord, just as others help me with a new start,
I pray that you will use me this day to help others start anew in their relationships with you. Amen.

REFLECTION/ACTION

For me personally, a "new start" in Jesus Christ means . . . .
How can I make this "new start" more vivid in my own life and share it with others?

Morning—Day Twelve

In the Middle

READ: Genesis 12:1-3
Romans 12:9-13

This has been one heck of a day, Lord.
Every time I came around the corner, I ran into something half-finished.
Around the corner and bam. I found myself walking right into it.
A crying secretary, an overheated spouse, a distraught mother, an anxious boss, a tired janitor, a confused and overworked lawyer—there it was, Lord.
When do I begin, where can I start?
Why can't I ever seem to come in at the beginning?
But when I think about it, I realize that only you were at the beginning.
Since then people have been coming in "in the middle."
Even Jesus came in "in the middle."
To a world already distraught, Jesus came in "in the middle" of humankind's predicament.
Lord, give me the courage to come "in the middle," equipped with that same Word and love.
Make me be more concerned with the outcome than I am the beginning.
Let me just be glad I have been invited to be a part of the middle rather than nothing at all. Amen.

REFLECTION/ACTION

Out of the experiences I have had, one was a new beginning in spiritual life for me. Has this experience and others helped me to reach out and share with other persons?

Evening—Day Twelve

Pushy, Pushy, Pushy

READ: Luke 11:9-13

Lord God,
I found myself waking up at 4:50 a.m. this morning.
Already my mind was going ninety miles an hour, planning the day's activities and considering whether or not things had been taken care of at the office.
I wondered how people were going to react to my planning.
Sometimes I wonder why I push myself so hard.
I work as if your kingdom depended only on me.
Where did I ever get such an inflated ego, to think you depend only on me?
I am confused, Lord.
You do depend on me, don't you?
I guess I am convinced that you count on me.
My confusion stems from answering: Where does the initiative for this dependence come from?
Help me relax and stop relying so heavily on myself; instead, help me rely on your leading.
You have promised to go before us.
In my planning, considering, and wondering, help me have an eye fixed on you.
Make me listen to your voice of calling, and not to my voice of pushing.
It is in your service I seek to be,
in your presence I seek to live,
and it is in Christ's name I pray. Amen.

REFLECTION/ACTION

How could relying upon God, rather than myself, change my life? How would my life need to change if I decided right now to rely upon God more completely with my job, family, finances, and community?

Morning—Day Thirteen

Saved Through Grace

READ: Acts 15:6-11

Dear Lord,
Help me look at ways I have tried to get close to you.
Help me look at today.
Today I loved my brother;
  I cared for a widow;
  I spoke to a child;
  I prayed in your sanctuary;
  I shared the Good News with others;
  I ate and prayed in public places;
  I shared your love in service;
  I planned your program at the church;
  I served your body and blood in the chapel;
  I healed the hurts of words and actions;
  I witnessed the Lamb with people in need;
  I gave food to the hungry;
  I visited the sick in hospitals.
Now it comes to me, as I look up the page.
As I recalled the day, everything was prefaced by "I."
"I" did everything.
It is the "I" that gets in the way.
It should be—you loved, you cared, you spoke, you prayed, you shared, you ate, you planned, you served, you healed, you witnessed, you gave, and you visited.
You did all these things through me. I was merely an agent for you.
In all my searching, in all my trying to get close to you, I found you already standing close to me. Amen.

REFLECTION/ACTION

Was I able to turn some new area of life over to God today? Did I find God standing close to me in some new way? I experienced God working through me to reveal, serve, care, and speak to others by . . .

Evening—Day Thirteen

Fools for Christ

READ: 2 Corinthians 11:12-30

Father God,
Sometimes, you call us in strange ways.
But would you really call us to be a fool?
Would you call us to get up before people and act foolish?
Aren't we to be dignified, reserved, and intelligent people?
Why would you want us to be fools?
I think many would rather dig a ditch, climb a skyscraper, or slop the pigs.
All those things we could do in the safety of solitude, not displaying ourselves before other people.
To be a fool and act foolish, we must stand before other people.
They will think less of us.
That is the point!
Seeing how foolish a dignified person can seem, gives reason to rely on God.
When we build our world and hopes, our kingdoms and future only on people, what fools!
O God, allow our foolishness to point to your sanity, so we might boast in your strength. Amen.

REFLECTION/ACTION

Why do I want to be a Christian? Am I able to risk appearing foolish in order to share my faith and the gospel with others?

Morning—Day Fourteen

Hope

READ: 1 Corinthians 15:35-58

Lord God,
Today the radio carried the story of over five hundred people being killed in an airplane collision.
There were also four rapes, two murders, and an assortment of traffic deaths.
The stock market is gyrating.
The Russians are belligerent, and revolutionaries are marching.
Wives and husbands are going their separate ways, and parents are chewing up their children at an alarming rate.
What is the answer?
When will it stop?
Will it catch me in the process?
Is there no hope in the world? Is there no hope for the world?
Father, I guess I have answered my own question.
"Hope" is not *in* the world.
"Hope" is Christ *for* the world.
When we bring a different kind of value, a different kind of promise, along with Christ to the world, we find hope.
Christ brings resurrection, and new life to the world.
Lord, help me see Christ's resurrection in the world and in me. Amen.

REFLECTION/ACTION

The mystery that the resurrection unfolds is hope. All of us face despair at one time or another, but there is always the promise of hope. There is no situation in existence to which Christ cannot bring hope. When have I experienced hope or resurrection in a new way?

Evening—Day Fourteen

Anger

READ: Matthew 5:21-26

Almighty Lord,
Blessed is the day when I can come to you, opening my heart before you and asking that you help me examine my life.
Help me this day, I pray, Lord, to understand anger.
Things can happen between two people and before you know it there are words, feelings, emotions, division, and hurt.
Each goes his separate way.
Victims of despair live in anguish that holds them inactive, eats at their faith, and hinders even their vision of you.
Lord, help me understand that anger begins when I put myself first.
"I know the facts." "I see things more clearly."
"You are wrong."
Help me to put you first.
Help me to put others second.
Help me to put myself third.
That is the only way to overcome anger. Amen.

REFLECTION/ACTION

Forgiveness is at the center of reconciliation and the resolution of anger. Do I find it difficult to forgive?
Do I find it difficult to accept forgiveness? Today I will try to make the first steps toward reconciliation between myself and someone from whom I feel separated.

Morning—Day Fifteen

Listening

FOR PRAISE READ: Psalm 107:1-9
FOR CONFESSION READ: Psalm 38:18-22

Dear Lord,
You have given me the parable of the sower and in patience explained its meaning.
Your word is all about me, seeking soil for growth and nurture.
Teach me to listen.
A small child, timid and afraid, with tears streaming down her face, comes seeking comfort and love.
Make my heart listen to her.
Make the words I speak be listening words that show your love.
An angry man came to my office.
Cheated by life's riches, he was poor, lonely, and angry with the way the world had controlled his life.
Make me listen and not continue to control him with my words.
Make me listen with understanding and respond to his needs.
Make me listen with the hope of your love.
A shattered marriage came upon my doorstep, onewayness going in two separate directions.
Years of ego and self-love were displayed in rage.
Help me listen until the couple hears faith speak, faith that is found only in Christ. In his name we pray. Amen.

REFLECTION/ACTION

Did I come to reconciliation with someone today? How did I feel?
How much success did I have in asking for forgiveness?

Evening—Day Fifteen

I Will Follow

READ: Romans 5:1-11

Eternal Father,
Sometimes I get up in the morning, with my whole day planned.
Schedules, meetings, duties, responsibilities, resources, talents, friends, colleagues, intuition, insight, hunches, and luck, just to name a few of the plans.
There are a lot of things that will influence me today.
There are a lot of things that I will count on today, Lord.
I will count on myself, others, even material things.
I will count on these in times of stress, joy, and celebration.
I will seek persons to help, to join, or to confirm me.
Sometimes, I will even give up and try to start anew seeking some new plateau of security.
What folly I seek.
I know there is only One I should trust.
You know where I have been.
You know where I stand.
And you know where I should go.
Lead me, O Father, and I will follow. Amen.

REFLECTION/ACTION

People are funny about the things in which they place trust: cars, jobs, and friends. We trust or have faith that nearly everything will work just as it has before. These are the things in which I have "faith". . .

Morning—Day Sixteen

Trials

READ: James 1:2-15

Dear Lord,
There is a contemporary song that goes something like this: "All my trials, Lord, will soon be over!"
I can remember the wailing tune.
Sometimes it plays over and over like a stuck record: Soon be over, soon be over, soon be over.
Why is it that I think that some day all of my trials will be over?
Life is searching, demanding, and testing.
There is no way I can escape it.
There is no way I cannot make choices.
Becoming a Christian and living a life of faith does not get me out of all that.
As a matter of fact, sometimes it makes me more aware.
Yet, being a Christian has equipped me with the tools to handle trials.
O Lord, help me to understand this privilege.
Send your Holy Spirit so that I will be equipped for all of the trials.
Give me your wisdom so I can work in the trials; give me a friend to walk with me through them.
Make me see you and praise you after the trials are over.
In your holy name, I pray. Amen.

REFLECTION/ACTION

How have experiences of trials made me grow stronger in faith? Have these experiences created problems I have been unable to reconcile in my faith?

Evening—Day Sixteen

And the Word Became Flesh

READ: Matthew 25:31-46

Dear Lord,
Help me to understand the great mystery of the Word becoming flesh.
When Jesus was born, your Word became flesh and dwelled among us, so that I could know you.
How do I know you today?
How do I experience the love that Jesus shared?
How do the lame walk again?
How are the multitudes fed on a hillside?
How do little children enter into the kingdom?
These are big questions.
You have given me the answer, but too many times I have denied it.
I have refused to accept your answer.
Jesus has said: "When you have done it to one of the least."
God, you have called me to be your flesh, speak your words, feed the hungry, and love the lonely.
Send forth your Spirit and I will be empowered to be your Word.
I humbly seek to be your servant. Amen.

REFLECTION/ACTION

"The Word became flesh" creates some particular images for me. From these images I find ways that I might share this Word with others.

Morning—Day Seventeen

Prayer

READ: Luke 3:21-22

Eternal Father,
Help me slow down.
I find myself approaching you with the wrong attitude.
I am saying to myself, "Now let's hurry up and get this over. I have so much to do."
We are all busy people, and there is so much to do.
But how good will the job be if I take the wrong tools to do it.
I find myself rushing to you, sometimes not only with the questions but with the answers.
Teach me to slow down and listen.
Do not allow me to just bring you all my problems and then go away tackling them myself.
Help me understand that prayer is waiting in silence, expecting to hear your word.
Dear Lord, come into my life and make a difference.
Make a difference in my response to all the opportunities you give me to speak of the salvation of Jesus Christ. Amen.

REFLECTION/ACTION

Life is such a rush these days; I need to slow down and listen. I find myself answering another person's question, even before they have finished asking? Sometimes I even do this with God. The scripture reading witnesses to the fact that as Jesus prayed, God's Spirit descended on him. In my waiting and listening, I will try to let God's Spirit descend upon me today.

Evening—Day Seventeen

Children of God

READ: Isaiah 56:6-7
Mark 3:31-35

Dear Lord,
Forgive me.
Yesterday a vagrant came to me and asked for help.
I turned him away with a terrible attitude.
I said to myself, "What responsibility do I have for him?"
We spend a lifetime building up walls that define the limits of our responsibility.
Oh, he's not a member of my church, he's not a member of my family, and he's not a member of my social club.
We try to justify our response to the human needs of others.
If their need could be called spiritual, maybe then we could fulfill it.
Lord, help us to understand that all children are your children.
Whoever does the will of God, seeks the will of God, or stands in need of the will of God is our responsibility.
All children, youth, men, and women have that need.
Help me call on your Spirit to dwell in my heart, so I can respond to the needs of your children. Amen.

REFLECTION/ACTION

Am I able to handle someone else's problems along with my own? Have I turned away because someone does not fit or belong neatly among those whom I consider my associates? Today, I will try to add *one* person to my family circle, love them, pray for them, and help bring the fulfillment of God's Spirit into their life.

Morning—Day Eighteen

Seeking The Rock

READ: Luke 18:9-14

Dear Lord,
There is one television commercial that intrigues me.
You know the one: everyone goes around saying they have a piece of the "rock."
That is very insightful, Lord.
But I am not sure other people understand the words in the way I understand them.
Lord, you know I come from very humble beginnings.
As a youth I worried about security, a financial guarantee that would protect me when I reached an age of non-production.
At times I still think about it and plan.
But at least now it's not a threat that demands much of my time.
I have come to a new understanding and a realization that I have a piece of the rock—the rock that represents real security, knows no sinking sand, and is called faith in Jesus Christ.
Now that's a piece of the rock!
It does not suffer inflation or devaluation.
It does not rust and thieves cannot break in and steal it.
It does not give one a false sense of self-valuation.
But it brings us humbly to our knees saying:
"Thank you, Lord, for your Son." Amen.

REFLECTION/ACTION

When I feel insecure, I believe that there is nothing in which I can place trust. However, when I come face to face with God, who is the ultimate in trust, love, and power, I find that God can give me all the security I will ever need. Then I wonder when was the last time I brought anyone to a new sense of security by sharing my faith?

Evening—Day Eighteen

Hitch Your Wagon to A Star

READ: Joel 2:27-29

Lord God,
I can remember my mother always telling me,
"Hitch your wagon to a star."
She would always add, "The star that shone over the manger."
I guess that was her way of saying: Set your sights on God, go with God, and he will go with you.
Father God, how can I develop a lifestyle that reflects a close relationship with you?
What can I do to enhance my life, as well as represent you to those I meet?
Much of my life is spent in making decisions.
Could I daydream a moment longer over each decision and ask, "Does this hook up with my star?"
Daydreams can be a time for thinking of ideals.
Let me daydream ways to be your disciple.
Lord, let your star shine so brightly in my life that I will constantly seek to hook every part of my life to it. For it is in Jesus' name I pray. Amen.

REFLECTION/ACTION

The day of the Lord comes to me when I realize and rely on his Spirit to direct, inform, and reveal his presence in my life. Dreaming and daydreaming can be a method by which God communicates to me. As I go about my daily tasks I need to ask, "Is this of God?" How could my lifestyle make me conscious of God's presence in my life?

Morning—Day Nineteen

Blessed Are the Meek

READ: Romans 7:13-20
Romans 8:5-11

Lord,
How many times have I refused you today?
Sometimes hiding, sometimes denying, but most of the time just being quiet.
Why do Christians feel so intimidated by the world?
I can remember my grandmother—she was a small lady.
Toward the end of her life, you might even say she was frail.
But that only speaks of her physically.
What about her soul?
I just keep remembering the scripture: "Blessed are the meek."
So many times in her life she was able to witness through her meekness.
Quiet, but strongly committed and never varying in her relationship, in her response, in her witness to her faith in you.
Lord, teach me to be meek—
not meekness that hides, but meekness that speaks clearly. Amen.

REFLECTION/ACTION

Some experiences of my day will remain part of my memory for a long time. Why are they significant? Did they force me to grow closer to God? Am I more aware of God's presence?

Evening—Day Nineteen

I Love To Teach

READ: Romans 12:1-13

Dear Lord,
I love to teach in your ministry; there is something exhilarating about sharing the wisdom of the ages.
Lord, I thank you for all your teachers who have shared their insight, experience, and faith; so that we can better know and affirm our faith.
Lord, I love the challenge of questions.
Questions portray the search that is inside each of us, as we seek to know you more fully.
Lord, let there never be a day in my life that I do not have at least one question for you.
Lord, I love the celebration of an answer—when people's souls are finally awakened to some new vista or glance of you.
That great "aha!"
Lord, let there never be a day in my life when I do not get at least one new glance of you.
Lord, I love the peace of affirmation.
It is magnificent when a company of your committed can stand together and say: "This I believe."
Help me, Lord, always to find fellowship in that company which is committed to you. Amen.

REFLECTION/ACTION

How often have I hesitated to ask a question just because I thought it was "a dumb question"? I have been in meetings when people have said, "Now this is going to be a dumb question, but. . .?" Sometimes those dumb questions cut to the heart of a problem or opportunity. Today, I will take courage, go ahead, and ask those questions and see that it will increase communication. Those "dumb" questions have helped me . . .

Morning—Day Twenty

I Can Give

READ: Matthew 5:38-42

Today Lord,
I was driving through the south end of town.
It was a warm and sunny day, and the streets were lined with beggars.
They were joking and having a good time with each other.
But each time a stranger passed by, they would ask for food, or money, or both.
Lord, how many times in my life have I been asked for
food and money,
shelter and guidance,
care and love,
truth and salvation?
What has been my answer?
How have I met the challenge?
Lord, have I gazed into your eyes when I have
looked the beggar in the face,
wiped away the tears of a young widow,
spoken to a confused youth,
shared with my own children?
Lord, have I turned back on you?
Help me use my life as a witness to the love, and the life of Jesus, as I try to answer the needs of those around me. Amen.

REFLECTION/ACTION

Has anyone in need ever asked me for food, money, or shelter? Was that all they really wanted? What would I give away? I can give away whatever special gift God has given me—money, time, special talent, care, and love. I wonder, what would that do for my faith?

Evening—Day Twenty

Sacrifice

READ: Genesis 22:1-19
Hebrew 11:17-18

Father God,
In this day of plenty, we seemed to have lost sight of what it means to sacrifice.
In a world of *more* and *have,* we have forgotten how to *save* and *sacrifice.*
You asked Abraham to sacrifice his son Isaac as proof and test of his faith.
Sometimes we think it would be easier if you aked us to give ourselves, and not ask for our beloved children.
Lord, what we do not realize is that maybe you are asking us to sacrifice ourselves. We just do not realize it.
You ask us to sacrifice through the
eyes of the hungry,
hearts of the lonely,
longings of young minds,
aching of the aged,
giving of ministry.
Lord, send your Spirit, so our hearts are so confirmed that we can sacrifice again.
You have given your Son as sacrifice.
Help me understand what you are asking me to sacrifice. Amen.

REFLECTION/ACTION

Where does sacrifice fit into my personal faith? Am I able to sacrifice for God and his work?

Morning—Day Twenty-one

Spring Day

READ: 1 Peter 2:1-10

Eternal Creator,
Today I have encountered you in many ways.
When I first went out this morning, there you were in the bright, clear yellow crocus.
When I dug deep in the garden's soil, there you were in the smell of the humus.
When I dropped the seeds in the straight furrow, there you were in the promise of the harvest.
As I went to the busy office, there you were in the needs of a mother, a traveler, and a priest.
When I responded to a call for help, here you were in care and love.
On bended knee in the chapel, I felt you saying: "Your sins are forgiven."
Lord, there is no place I can go, or any place I care to go, where you are not already there.
You are there willing and waiting to help me.
As I open myself up to you,
I find cleansing first, and then great joy because of your presence.
Lord, bring me again and again to a realization that every aspect of life is yours.
Touch my life everywhere. Amen.

REFLECTION/ACTION

Have I given myself completely to God's work? How can I continue to give myself more and more completely to God's work? Has my awareness of God's presence in my life grown greater as I have increased my willingness to give myself to him?

Evening—Day Twenty-one

READ: [illegible]

Dear God,
That alarm this morning was [illegible]
[illegible]

[illegible]

Checking in God

READ: Ephesians 5:1-13

Dear God,
That alarm this morning was beastly loud.
Some mornings it jars me right out of bed.
Why, Lord, does it bother me so, and other mornings it is a clarion call to a new life?
This serves to make me wonder what happens elsewhere.
Down the street at John and Betty's house, do they wake up to soft music?
Across the street at Tim and Joyce's, do they wake up to the cry of their small child?
Or across the river at Dale and B. J.'s, do they wake up to the bark of a dog, the demand of a child, the ring of the alarm, or the call of your Spirit?
The call of your Spirit.
Some people get up in the morning checking the clock, some checking the weather, and some check the stock market.
Some people check the school menu, others check their horoscope, and still others check their tea leaves.
But Lord, what would it be like if all your children got up in the morning checking their spirit?
What if all people checked to see if your Spirit was within them?
Glory, what a daybreak that would be! Amen.

REFLECTION/ACTION

When I got up today was I aware of God's presence in me? What can I do for God today? I pray I will walk in God's presence.

Morning—Day Twenty-two

Chatter

READ: Psalm 62

Heavenly Father,
I am home at last and in the silence of the night, I can turn to you.
My ears are ringing from talk, talk, talk!
Moment by moment my day was punctuated by words, chatter, and talk.
Some was understandable and meaningful, but most was needless, aimless, blatting talk with no purpose, no content, and no objective.
There were words that hurt, talk that was tart and cutting, and chatter that was childish and needless.
Lord, help me again to realize the beauty of words and the meaningfulness of heart-to-heart talks.
You speak a "word" and it "is."
Help me draw so near you that once again I can speak words of truth.
Help me again share love with my words, and Christ with my words.
Lord, help me enhance the meaningfulness of words with appropriate silence.
But when I speak, let my speech be truthful. Amen.

REFLECTION/ACTION

I have failed to share with anyone many of my experiences with God. I can remember one experience in particular when I . . .

Evening—Day Twenty-two

Me—I—Me

READ: Romans 6:1-14

Lord God,
Help me! Help me. Help me?
So much of my day is filled with "My," "I," and "Me."
I catch myself making decisions based totally on what I want, what suits me, and what keeps things mine.
I fall into the trap of thinking that the world was built for me.
The way of the world is the way of conflict.
I get caught up in the world of decisions, and it traps and ensnares me to assert myself.
It seems I must always speak for myself, stand up for myself, state where I stand on the issues.
God, give me the presence of mind always to consider peace, love, and your way when I make decisions.
Liberate me from thinking my way and make me a spokeman for your way.
Help me resolve conflict by sharing the wisdom of your peace.
Help me dissolve walls of hatred by sharing your love in moments of care.
Help me to become a new creature, that calls forth the new creature in each of your children. Amen.

REFLECTION/ACTION

As a Christian I am asked to consider things from outside my particular point of view. I am asked to consider things from God's point of view. What would it mean for my life to consider things from God's point of view, rather than my own?

Morning—Day Twenty-three

Sleep, But No Rest

READ: Isaiah 51:1-6

Eternal Father,

How many times have I plunged my body down on my bed and slept heavily, but have found no rest.

I think of persons in a sprawling city—of ghetto, suburbs, and surrounding country.

Night after night they turn to their beds, hoping to find rest in their sleep.

Sleep comes—that state of arrested sight—but rest will not come.

In all the turning and tossing, in all the pain and sickness, in all the frustration and family fighting, people's minds and souls find no rest.

Maybe with sleeping pills, we humans can get out of our situation, but then morning thrusts us painfully back into reality.

Lord, help us realize that the only answer to anguish, the only answer to this painful soul is trust in you.

In that trust we find the eternal rest. Amen.

REFLECTION/ACTION

Has seeing things from God's point of view made me more able to resolve or avoid conflict today? When was the last time I did not force my own agenda on a situation and instead accepted God's agenda? What was the meaning of this experience?

Evening—Day Twenty-three

A New Covenant

READ: Matthew 26:26-29

Dear Lord,
My body is making new blood every moment of my life.
I have thought how similar this is to the New Covenant I can encounter in Christ.
You appeared to Abraham and blessed Abraham. By Abraham all people became blessed, as they entered into a covenant with you.
Jesus came asking people to enter into a New Covenant.
He called it a New Covenant because in each moment of life there are new opportunities to choose and affirm you to be my God.
There are also new opportunities for me to choose to be your disciple.
Each time a new decision comes along I have the opportunity to make a New Covenant with you in that decision.
It is my prayer: "Let the blood of Jesus be in my covenant and decisions." Amen.

REFLECTION/ACTION

How would it be if I allowed the blood of the New Covenant to flow freely in my veins? I will try to allow Christ to come alive in each one of my activities.

Morning—Day Twenty-four

Feed My Sheep

READ: James 2:14-26

Father God,
When I got up this morning, I had breakfast as routinely as breathing the next breath.
And when lunch's appointed time comes I shall eat.
Likely there will be a banquet this evening when I return home.
Food, food, food, for most Americans it is a way of life.
Food with meetings, food with visits, and food to go to bed by.
I have eaten enough in excess to keep two other people alive.
Where is my conscience?
Lord, help me to understand the needs of people around a hungry world.
No—do not make me only understand, make me do something about the needs of people around a hungry world.
Make me use this one life of mine to reach out to the needs of others, to help other people become aware of the need, enable the hungry to help themselves, quiet profit and answer need.
Lord, do not allow me to be content just to love, or to say I love those in need, and do nothing to answer their needs.
Help me and use me to feed your sheep with a love that answers their need. Amen.

REFLECTION/ACTION

We can be hungry in so many ways. I know, I have experienced some of the different hungers. How do I react when I see someone suffering from any kind of hunger? Where does my Christian faith fit?

Evening—Day Twenty-four

The Closed Door

READ: Colossians 1:15-29

Lord,
Here I am, already in my office, before 7:00 A.M., hard at your work.
Now, if I can only keep that door closed and keep people out of my hair, I will get some work done.
All of this work is for you, Lord. Right?
Wrong!
Why is it I find myself saying,
"If only these people would get out of my office, would leave me alone, would stop calling me at home, and would take care of themselves, I could get some work done."
But I must ask myself, what work?
What work is so important that it must go on behind closed doors, or cannot have the cares and needs of people at its heart.
Send your Spirit and your image, Jesus Christ, to me again and again; so I can see again how you meet people in their need, along dusty roads, and in the marketplaces.
It is in all of these places that you care and love them into a relation with you.
Help me, help others seek eternal life. Amen.

REFLECTION/ACTION

Sometimes I am convinced that if I do not have seclusion, closed doors, and no one bothering me that I cannot do my work. Yet, I am at the same time aware that Jesus did his work with, for, and among people. He was never behind closed doors. I wonder, could I work that way?

Morning—Day Twenty-five

Along the Road

READ: Luke 24:13-35

Heavenly Father,
Why is it so difficult to recognize you along the road?
We can recognize Tom, Jane, Anne, and Dick.
We can recognize a flat tire, a pothole in the road, a red light at the crossroad, or a Chevrolet Impala.
Why is it we do not recognize you?
In the coming days, help me to recognize you in
the stranger's look of loneliness,
a child's glance revealing a potential that needs guidance,
a mother's seeking for affirmation, "Am I doing right?"
a teenager's search for "help me be!"
Make me recognize that you gave yourself to others in an affirming way.
Help me reveal you to others in an affirming way.
In Christ we ask it, and in Christ we find it. Amen.

REFLECTION/ACTION

Did I find Christ walking the "dusty road to Emmaus" today? Was Christ alive in my relationships? Where did Christ walk the dusty road with me today?

Evening—Day Twenty-five

Dancing Spirit

READ: Psalm 150

Dear Lord,
When I was a teenager, I never could get the beat.
The twist, the jerk, and the shuffle were all the latest dances.
I sat on the sidelines; I was a real square.
Lord, help my squareness.
On the other hand, my four-year-old daughter is a real swinger.
Everytime music comes on the radio, she pulsates with the beat.
Why is it so easy for some to dance?
Help me to dance.
There are those whose dance is slowed because of hunger, hopelessness, precedence, or handicap.
Help me, Lord, to quicken their step with the Good News.
And there are those whose dance does not match the music because of broken homes, confused priorities, or different lifestyles.
Help me, Lord, to teach them the step of acceptance.
And to those who do not come to the dance because of injured esteem, fragmented identities, or lack of hope, help me, Lord, to take the dance to them.
Dance, dance, dance.
Father, teach us all to dance in your presence. Amen.

REFLECTION/ACTION

So many times my heart seems to know the joy of the presence of God, but my feet do not know the steps. Yet in sharing the Spirit of God with others, have I found that there is a dance I know?

Morning—Day Twenty-six

Labors

READ: Matthew 11:25-30

Eternal Father,
I do not know when I have worked such long hours.
I cannot remember when I have dealt with such exasperating problems, ministered to such broken lives, labored physically with so much detail, or tangled with so much opposition.
My body is tired.
My senses have been dulled.
The strength of my soul has been stretched.
Even my family has wearied from my schedule.
But, praise God!
You have not given me a task too great, nor challenged me without mercy.
You have called me to this ministry, and you have equipped me for the task.
I praise your holy name!
While broken lives have come to me, you have been there to heal them.
When anguished hearts have shared with me, you have brought hope to them again.
While tangled schedules have kept me apart from my family, you have shared your love with them.
What joy it is to know the comfortable feeling that your yoke brings to our lives, a joy received, a challenge met.
It is the comfortable feeling of a job well done, a challenge met, a light of hope rekindled, a heart warmed with love.
Father, never let my life be idle.
I come to know your joy when I am asked to wear your yoke. Amen.

REFLECTION/ACTION

Was I able to share a "dance" of the Spirit with anyone today? Did anything get in the way of my dancing? Why did some of the tasks facing me today seem so impossible? Did I sense God working through me in the events of the day?

Evening—Day Twenty-six

A Simple Touch

READ: Mark 10:13-31

Father God,
All is quiet here in my study.
The sun is rising and that red tint of the sky is awakening the song of the birds.
My cat is purring so loudly that it sounds like a drum.
A leaf scratching against the window is keeping time with the pulse of the earth.
So often we pass up the simple gifts you have given us.
Are there other more important things?
No! Life has just become drugged with bizarre, multimotion activities.
Even when we approach you in prayer it is always,
"Here I stand, your prophet, your priest, your lawyer,
your church official."
No, no, no! It never seems to be,
"Here I stand, your child."
Help me to seek the simplicity of a child.
The honesty of a child overwhelms me.
"Dad, you've got bad breath."
"That frightens me."
"I don't like to be yelled at."
"I love you."
The touch of a child can feel so much.
The honesty of a child can heal so much.
The hope of a child can restore so much.
A child's love can change so much.
God, scrub away the years of age, so I can again be childlike and rely on simple touch.
You are touching my heart with love.
Help me become your disciple of the simple touch. Amen.

REFLECTION/ACTION

I know there is wisdom in sharing God's abundant love in different ways. What are some simple ways I can share God's love?

Morning—Day Twenty-seven

Throwaway World

READ: Matthew 25:14-30

At the end of the week, I find myself in the garage tying newspapers, sweeping up dirt, and bagging the garbage.
Is this my offering for the week's efforts?
This world is becoming a throwaway world.
I have in my reach throwaway cups, plates, cake pans, clothes, car parts, house parts, contracts, commitments, marriages, rites, idols, and gods.
If there is anything wrong with it—cracked, marred, used, cheated, inflexible, just, challenging, confronting, honest, or decent—I have no use for it and throw it away.
Honesty is too challenging to stand next to.
Justice is too challenging a way to relate.
Decency is too challenging to live by.
Forgive me, Father, for the way I have used your grace.
You have given me a measure of grace—the grace of knowing, sharing, hoping, and loving.
Do not let me squander your gifts by investing and participating in a throwaway world. Help me instead to enhance the gifts of grace you have given so that I might move to the permanent things of life. Write your love permanently in my heart. Amen.

REFLECTION/ACTION

God has given us much that is not throwaway, unless we choose to throw it away. He has given us love, music, sharing, other persons, and on and on. What are some things God has given me which should be kept and used rather than thrown away?

Evening—Day Twenty-seven

New Life

READ: Acts 2:22-28

Father God,
I need a rebirth or a new start.
Life gets so complicated and so hectic.
Life is a maze of entanglements and contradictions.
If we allow it to happen, all the troubles of the world can build up and weigh us down.
What can be the answer to a situation like mine?
What can be the answer to a situation like the world?
Is it trust in you? Are you in control?
Hallelujah! You are in control!
Your will is in the world and it is your will that it shall be done.
You would not call on me to do anything I could not do.
If a mountain seems too high, I am not relying on your Spirit and strength.
If other people's problems seem too many, then "I" must stop trying to handle them.
I must let you handle them.
Jesus Christ—he is faith and hope alive in the world.
He is the Savior of the world, and not me.
New life comes through an encounter with your son Jesus Christ.
New life comes when I again trust in you.
Thank you for the problems in my life.
Once again, realizing my own weaknesses I have turned to your strength and received *new life.* Amen.

REFLECTION/ACTION

Rebirth can happen in our life every time we let Christ be revealed in our lives—through loving, hearing the world cares, and turning our wills and lives over to God. We have the greatest opportunity in the world to make specific Christ's love in the world. What opportunities will I have to make Christ specific in my own life, as well as in the lives of others?

Morning—Day Twenty-eight

Judging

READ: Matthew 7:1-5

Father God,
I have dealt unjustly with my neighbor.
I have quickly told him where he is wrong.
Yet, I have hardly dealt with my own shortcomings:
"I cannot get this done because he . . .;"
"I would be the greatest but they. . . ."
Funny? No! It is tragic how I have built a world that rotates around myself.
If I did not see it, it did not happen.
If I did not approve it, then it has no authority.
Based on the facts I have, I judge, as if I have to see all things, know all facts, and analyze all factual, psychological, and emotional evidence.
Father, cure my judging tendency.
Get me out of the center of the universe, and help me put you back in the position I have been assuming for myself.
Set me to the task of finding all those neighbors I have wronged.
Help me humbly to ask their forgiveness.
Make me own the faults I have blamed them for, and help me confess my faults to you.
Do not let me disown my faults any longer by saying they belong to someone else.
My life stands in your judgment.
That is all the judgment that I, or my brothers and sisters, need. Amen.

REFLECTION/ACTION

In Hebrew "to judge" conveys more than the corresponding English term. The act of judging makes right a wrong either by punishment of the aggressor or by restitution to the victim, and sometimes both. Judgment is the realization of justice. In New Testament terms, God judges us sinful, renders the verdict, then he is responsible for justice by sending Christ. How does the scripture's version of justice relate to what we call justice in our world?

Evening—Day Twenty-eight

Let the Children

READ: Matthew 18:1-4

Father God,
I marvel at the faith of my daughter.
There seem to be no gray areas in her life when it comes to trust in you.
This experience has taught me something about faith.
Help me understand the difference between faith and knowledge, information and skill.
Time and time again I find myself relying on my knowledge, my skill, or the information I possess, instead of my faith.
Help me become like a child, and see the caterpillars among all the leaves of the forest, or hope for the rainbow at the end of the storm, and love the funny little man at the end of the block.
Help me to put my hand in yours,
walk with you in the face of cares, and carry you in the midst of need and hurt.
Help me recapture the mystery of my daughter's faith,
for to such faith belongs the keys to the kingdom of heaven.
Make me, like a child, dwell in your kingdom. Amen.

REFLECTION/ACTION

Jesus tells us true greatness comes when we turn away from self-chosen goals and relate to God as a father. Childlike relations to a parent, not childish behavior, are the beginnings of faith. Is childlike trust a part of my faith? Am I able to trust and be God's disciple?

Morning—Day Twenty-nine

Barbed Wire

READ: Psalm 136

Heavenly Father,
I hate barbed wire!
No matter how cautiously I walk around it, it reaches out and grabs me.
Even if I try to step over it, it grabs me by the seat of the pants.
If I try to crawl carefully between it, it snags my shirttail.
Why is there barbed wire in my life?
Life seems like a barbed wire fence—some people, situations, ministries, are like a barbed wire fence.
No matter how carefully I approach them, they grab me by the seat of my pants.
Regardless of how carefully I try to word what I say to a particular lady, she jumps all over me like the odor from a skunk.
I cannot help but put my foot in my mouth.
Some people's problems are like trying to go through a barbed wire fence.
Regardless of how carefully you word a suggestion in the face of need, it goes wrong.
The needful person reaches out and grabs you.
That person often finds the right answer for the wrong question.
I hate barbed wire, except when there is a bull on the other side of it. Amen.

REFLECTION/ACTION

I have often been caught in the barbed wire of life. Sometimes I get so snagged and caught I loose control. How can I cope?

Evening—Day Twenty-nine

The Sabbath

READ: Exodus 16:22-30

And on the seventh day, Lord, you called us to rest and give praise.
Whatever happened to that day of rest?
Oh, some still rest and some play, but for the most part people treat Sunday just like any other day.
They do not remember their praise for you.
Lord, help me to remember the sabbath, a day of confessing, praising, singing, laughing, loving, and living in your presence.
I know if I can develop a lifestyle that remembers you on the sabbath, then I have made the first small step of bringing you into all of my life.
As I remember the sabbath you will be near and become dear to me.
Remembering the sabbath I will have started the trip that puts you in my loving, giving, praising, and confessing.
You will be in all my living.
Make me always have the grace to remember it on Sundays and all the days of my life.
In pursuit of your love. Amen.

REFLECTION/ACTION

The Exodus was a trying experience for the Hebrews. Forty years of wandering in the wilderness brought the Hebrews face to face with every situation that can be imagined. The significance of the event in the lives of the Hebrews was that they learned to trust in God. There was no problem so great, or opportunity so challenging, that God was not in the midst of it providing strength and hope. Where is my "Exodus?" And on whom am I relying to get through it? I need to witness to others about the trust I have found in the Lord.

Morning—Day Thirty

Hope for Tomorrow

READ: Matthew 5:14

Father God,
What a magnificent day!
Full of your loving, full of your living, full of your spirit.
Why is it, Lord, that so much of the time I am prone to look at the worst things in my life.
I focus on the killing, cheating, egotistic side of people.
Help me raise my sights.
Help me to find my hope in your Son.
How much time do we really spend looking at your model for our lives?
We read the newspaper daily.
We watch TV daily.
We listen to another person's side of life daily.
Help us each day to put some hope in our lives, through prayer, reading the scriptures, and encountering your Son Jesus.
In Jesus there is hope for change in our lives.
In Jesus there is hope for love in our lives.
In Jesus there is hope for life in our lives. Amen.

REFLECTION/ACTION

It is true we have gained great knowledge. The secrets of God's universe are being revealed to us through knowledge. We can split the atom. We can go to the moon. We can travel the veins of a person's blood system as if we were in a submarine. We can create a human with any color eyes, hair, and complexion we may choose. God's will is being unfolded to us in ways we never would have dreamed. Have we the moral maturity to handle the intellectual knowledge we now possess? I must evaluate my faith development as compared to my intellectual and social development. What can I continue to do that will help my faith to grow to its greatest possible maturity?

Evening—Day Thirty

This has been a thirty-day experiment in journal writing. You have been guided with scriptures and prayers. You have been challenged by actions that grew out of reflection upon Christ's presence in your family, your business, and your own personal life. But this is only the beginning.

I hope you will continue keeping a journal. Use the introduction of this book, referring to it frequently to test how your journal writing is going. Adapt the format to fit your time schedule, your devotional style, and your spiritual needs. But by all means, find some way to continue this heart-to-heart talk with God and yourself about your spiritual formation.